SOUTH
Ghost

Prepare to be frightened by these terrifying
tales from around South Wales

BRADWELL
BOOKS

Published by Bradwell Books
9 Orgreave Close Sheffield S13 9NP
Email: books@bradwellbooks.co.uk

British Library Cataloguing in Publication Data: a catalogue
record for this book is available from the British Library.
1st Edition
ISBN: 9781902674452

Print: Gomer Press, Llandysul, Ceredigion SA44 4JL

Design by: JenksDesign
Photographs credited individually

CONTENTS

INTRODUCTION

South Wales has it all: glorious countryside, a stunning coastline, rich heritage and a vibrant 'capital city'. Its attractiveness to day-trippers and holidaymakers has long been recognised. South Wales boasts the first place to be designated an Area of Outstanding Natural Beauty – the Gower Peninsula – and two National Parks: the Pembrokeshire Coast and the Brecon Beacons. History buffs come to marvel at the astonishing number of medieval castles in the region (more per square mile than anywhere else in the UK).

South Wales has a darker heritage, too. Its ghostly heritage. Almost every one of its dozens of ruined castles, for example, are said to be haunted. Then there are its numerous haunted mansions, pubs and hotels. Ghosts may be encountered, too, out of doors. Roads, lanes, fields, hillsides, caves, even the beaches may boast a ghost or two. Some of these spooks are of great antiquity, dating back to the Dark Ages, perhaps even into prehistory. Others are delightfully modern. Whatever their origin, many seem to be as active now as they've ever been. You have a better chance of seeing (or hearing) a ghost in South Wales than most places.

I hope this book encourages you to explore this haunted heritage for yourself. In doing so you will also find yourself visiting some of the most interesting and beautiful locations in South Wales.

HAUNTED CASTLES

South Wales is sometimes referred to as 'The Land of Castles' because of the great number of medieval fortresses strung out across its landscape. Most date from the period of the Norman occupation in the 11th and 12th centuries. Many of them are haunted, a number with legends dating back to that turbulent time in the history of Wales. In this chapter I'll highlight the ghost stories attached to those castles which are today most worth visiting (the majority are in the care of the heritage body for Wales, Cadw: http://cadw.wales.gov.uk).

Caerphilly

This magnificent ruin with its distinctive 'leaning tower' is the haunt of 'the Green Lady', a woman of the medieval period dressed, as her name suggests, in a green gown. One account suggests she is a grotesque creature, a small woman with an outlandishly large head and 'goggle eyes' which glow a fierce red. Knights in armour sometimes accompany her as she patrols the walls. Another weird creature, the Gwrach y Rhibyn, used to haunt marshy ground beneath the castle (see the final chapter, 'The Gloomiest Ghosts of All' for more).

Caerphilly Castle, with its distinctive 'leaning tower', is the haunt of a weird lady dressed all in green.

Cardiff (Caerdydd)

Cardiff Castle, which is open to the public, is haunted by the 2nd Marquess of Bute, who died suddenly in 1848 after a dinner party. The ghost of a young woman in a long trailing gown has also been seen but her identity is a mystery. On the drive leading up to the castle a phantom coach has been both seen and heard. It is believed to haunt when a member of the house of Hastings dies (Lady Sophia Bute was a member of the family of the Marquesses of Hastings).

Magnificent Cardiff Castle has a long history of ghostly phenomena.
Photo © Cardiff Council

A phantom lady in grey has been seen at this bridge waving frantically up to the massive walls of Cardiff Castle.

The Grey Lady is another famous ghost of Cardiff: she has been seen walking past the castle down to the bridge over the river, where she turns and waves. It is thought she is the apparition of a woman waving to a loved one who may have been imprisoned in the castle in its feudal days (www.cardiffcastle.com).

Carew

A strange legend is attached to Carew Castle in Pembrokeshire. In the early 17th century the castle was owned by Sir Roland Rhys, an ill-tempered and debauched individual with a reputation for treating his tenants abominably. Among his more peculiar characteristics was his fondness for a pet ape which he

A beauty and a beast haunt the ruins of Carew Castle.

kept in the castle. It was a vicious brute and Sir Roland enjoyed setting it on unfortunate underlings. One of his victims was a Flemish man named Horwitz, who had come to the castle to complain that Sir Roland's son had seduced his daughter. Refusing to believe the charge, Sir Roland accused Horwitz of slander and released the ape as punishment. The unfortunate man was left battered and bleeding by the creature and he crawled home more dead than alive.

That night Horwitz was awakened from a fitful slumber by a series of unearthly screams and howls from the direction of the castle. He dragged himself out of bed and went to investigate. The night sky was lit by a ruddy glow – Carew Castle was on fire! No one knows how the fire started or what exactly happened that night but Sir Roland's badly mauled body was found lying among the smouldering timbers. Crushed beneath a beam was the corpse of the ape, with blood upon its fangs and claws.

According to Pembrokeshire folk tales collector Brian John the ghosts of Sir Roland and his ape now haunt the castle ruins. He writes: 'To this day local people talk of terrible sounds disturbing the dead of night and echoing round the castle walls.'

A much less sinister ghost also haunts Carew, that of Nest, a 12th-century princess whose extraordinary beauty earned her the name of 'The Helen of Wales'. Her graceful figure has been seen sashaying among the ruins. Unusually she tends to appear in broad daylight rather than at night.

Castell Coch

Castell Coch – the Red Castle – is perched in a spectacular wooded location north of Cardiff and looks more like a French chateau than a British fortress. This is because it was rebuilt in the 19th century long after the original medieval castle had become a ruin. Tradition has it that a fabulous treasure was secreted away in the bowels of the original fortress and that it is guarded by huge, fierce supernatural eagles.

The French-style chateau of Castell Coch was set up in the 19th century over medieval ruins. It has inherited the original castle's ghosts.

During the Civil War more valuables were hidden at Castell Coch, this time by a nobleman loyal to King Charles I. He was killed in the Civil War before he had time to recover his money and still haunts the place, a sad elderly man in the rig-out of a Cavalier. Both hoards remain undiscovered to this day.

The original Norman fortress of Castell Coch engraved in the year 1860.
Two lots of treasure were buried here – both with supernatural guardians.

Kidwelly (Cidweli)

This Carmarthenshire castle, with its impressive gatehouse, has two ghosts, both dating from the Norman Conquest of England and Wales. They are the spirits of two women, one of whom welcomed the invaders and one of whom tired to repel them.

The Princess Gwenllian did her best to fight off the Normans when she found herself in possession of the original Welsh castle in the absence of her husband, Gruffydd ap Rhys ap Tudor. The brave lady was eventually captured and executed, however. The leader of the victorious Norman army, Maurice de Londres,

The massive gatehouse hints at the importance of Kidwelly Castle to the Norman conquest of Wales. Its two ghost stories both date from this turbulent time.

ordered that Gwenllian be beheaded as soon as the castle fell. Gwenllian's sad ghost is said to haunt Kidwelly, searching endlessly for her missing head.

Some years later, the beautiful Nest was one of the occupants of Kidwelly Castle. She was the daughter of the Lord of Kidwelly, Sir Elirdir Ddu, and was in love with a Norman baron, Sir Walter Mansel. Unfortunately, Sir Elirdir's niece Gwladys was also attracted to Sir Walter and was furiously jealous of the favours paid by the knight to Nest. To make matters worse, Nest's brother Griffith was vainly in love with Gwladys and was jealous of Sir Walter. This 12th century soap opera ended tragically.

When Sir Elirdir left for the Crusades, Griffith was left in charge and took matters into his own hands. Spurred on by the by now thoroughly spurned Gwladys, Griffith arranged for the murder of Sir Walter. The jealous Gwladys had spied on Nest and Sir Walter and knew that they liked to meet at a bridge over the river below the castle, away, as they thought, from prying eyes. An assassin hired by Griffith hid in the reed beds near the bridge and when Nest next met her lover there, he let an arrow fly, piercing Sir Walter's side. Sir Walter fell into the water and, with a horrified scream, Nest jumped in after him. Whether her intention was to try and save her lover or join him in death is unknown, but they both drowned.

Nest's spirit did not lie easy in her watery grave and she returned to haunt the living as a Ladi Wen, or White Lady, dressed in all in white and given to 'wild and unearthly shrieks'.

Manorbier

In his book *Pembrokeshire Folk Tales*, author Brian John reveals an interesting encounter with an apparition within the impressive ruins of Manorbier Castle. The incident took place during the

The looming walls of Manorbier Castle. During the First World War a soldier stationed here had the fright of his life.

First World War when soldiers were stationed on the castle's battlements to keep a watch out for enemy vessels along the coast. Usually two men were on duty at any one time but when a soldier fell ill one night it took some time for a replacement to be detailed. When the substitute made his way up to the castle he was surprised to find no one on duty. The other man had vanished. A search was made for him and he was eventually found unconscious on the village green. He had apparently jumped over a stream, leaving his rifle behind on the opposite bank, and then passed out.

When he came to, the unfortunate soldier had a very strange story to tell his superior officers. He said that after his fellow watchman had been taken ill, he had continued to patrol the battlements alone and then saw someone approaching him. It was a woman dressed all in white. He challenged her but still she came on. There was something so sinister about her that he finally fired a shot at her. But the bullet went straight through her. Then panic took over and the frightened soldier ran pell-mell for the safety of the village. It was presumed that in his panic he had dropped his rifle in jumping the stream and then fainted away from the shock.

Newport (Casnewydd)

The ghost of Newport Castle is a terrifying one – a huge, glaring giant in chain mail. It is thought to be the apparition of the first overlord of the castle, the Norman Robert FitzHamon, grown to giant size as befits his tyrannical status.

Another imposing Norman castle. Newport's ghost is as old as the battlements it patrols.

Ogmore (Castell Ogwr)

This Norman castle is situated down by the River Ogmore south of Bridgend. It is haunted by yet another White Lady, but one who has shown rather more spirit – if you'll pardon the pun – than the gentle ghosts of Kidwelly or Oystermouth.

This 'Ladi Wen' had the special charge of guarding a pot full of gold coins concealed beneath the floor of one of the castle's towers. One night a brave but foolish treasure-seeker sought out the ghost as she patrolled the castle ruins and convinced her to show him where the gold was hidden. As the man greedily ran the golden guineas through his fingers, the White Lady told him that he could take half the coins, but half only.

The treasure-seeker agreed and took half away. Some time later, though, greed got the better of him and he made a second nocturnal visit to the castle in order to help himself to the rest of the hoard. The White Lady was incensed and, accosting the man as he was tip-toeing away, laid into him with a vengeance. Armed with savage, claw-like fingernails, this ghostly femme fatale not only recovered her gold but left the thief in a terrible state, bleeding profusely, his clothes ripped to shreds. He never really recovered and died not long after.

Oystermouth (Ystum Llwynarth)

Another White Lady haunts this fortress on Gower near Swansea. She is the ghost of a beautiful and gracious Irishwoman who had been captured and forcibly married to the Norman baron then in control of Oystermouth, the Earl Neville. The pious and unhappy lady prayed that she be free for ever from the bonds of marriage to the brutal Earl Neville and her prayer was answered – the next morning she was found dead, 'like a saint, with hands folded on her breast'.

Since then Oystermouth Castle has been haunted by the White Lady. Some say she is to be seen in her former chamber above the gatehouse, others that she appears in the dungeon.

Traditional ghosts known as 'White Ladies' haunt many of the castles of Wales and Oystermouth is no exception.

Castle Roch photographed in the early 1900s. Unlike many of the original medieval castles of Wales, Roch is still habitable.

Roch

Roch Castle is one of the few that is not open to the public. Like St Donat's, below, it is still habitable and in private hands. Roch recently underwent a multi-million pound restoration programme and is to be used as a 'corporate retreat'. It's an impressive little fortress, perched on a crag in Pembrokeshire.

The well-known ghost of Roch Castle is Lucy Walter, a staunch Royalist who according to legend hurled a javelin at Oliver Cromwell during a Civil War siege. She was only fourteen at the time. She later became a mistress of Charles II, bearing him a son, James, who grew up to be the Duke of Monmouth. Sadly, Lucy died very young, abandoned and in poverty after leading something of a wild life.

Lucy is believed to have been born at Roch Castle, which is why the ghost has been so positively identified as her. However, like so many of the spooks haunting the castles of Wales, she is another 'Ladi Wen', a fair woman dressed all in white who drifts down the passages and through closed doors. The sound of running footsteps has also been reported, but whether they are related to the ghostly presence of Lucy Walter is uncertain.

By sheer number of ghosts alleged to have haunted here at one time or another, St Donat's can be considered the most haunted castle in Wales.

St Donat's

St Donat's Castle, near Llantwit Major, is better known today as Atlantic College, an international residential learning centre. Dating originally to the 14th century, it is wonderfully preserved but only open to the public for specific events.

Many ghost stories have been told about St Donat's. There are references to some really bizarre spooks, including a glowing eye and, of all things, the ghost of a panther! More orthodox is the ghost of Lady Stradling. She was a 17th-century member of the family who built the castle, and her ghost would appear all dressed up in her high heels and silk gown whenever death or some other calamity was shortly to befall a member of the Stradlings.

A traditional Welsh ghost, Mallt-y-Nos (which translates as 'Matilda of the Night'), is also said to haunt St Donat's. Matilda was a proud aristocrat who loved hunting so much that she once arrogantly proclaimed, 'If I cannot hunt in heaven I would rather not go there.' Now her restless spirit, debarred from heaven, rides through the night sky accompanied by a pack of the Welsh dogs of the underworld, the Cŵn Annwn.

A traitorous pirate who was murdered by his own crew haunts the beach below the castle walls. He was buried up to his neck and left struggling vainly as the tide came in.

HAUNT OF GHOST-HUNTERS

The lovely old house of Llancaiach Fawr (www.
llancaiachfawr.co.uk) can be found in the village of Nelson, not
far from Cardiff. Built in 1550, it is one of the best-preserved
Tudor mansions in Wales and is now a museum. In recent years,
with the growing popularity of organised ghost hunts following
in the wake of the *Most Haunted* television series, a great deal of
paranormal activity has been reported from Llancaiach Fawr
and it is often referred to as 'the most haunted house in Wales'.

The South Wales Paranormal Research group have carried out
numerous investigations at Llancaiach Fawr and detailed their
eerie results in a book, *Haunted Cardiff and the Valleys* (Tempus,
2007). Among the odd phenomena they and their guests have
experienced are loud knocks coming from various parts of the
mansion, an elusive aroma of 'flowery perfume' and a distinctive
'cold front' which sweeps down the staircase. On one occasion,
a male voice was heard in the apparently empty cellar asking
politely, 'How goes the day?'

Apparitions have also been seen by members of the SWPR. A
shadowy figure of a man in a tall hat has been glimpsed in the
kitchen. In an upstairs room, the Parlour, two apparitions were
seen during the same investigation. They could not have been
more different. One was described as a 'dark looming figure' of
threatening aspect but the other was of a pleasantly smiling lady
in a turquoise gown who, for the few seconds she was visible,

*The 16th century mansion of Llancaiach Fawr is one of the most haunted
houses in South Wales. Photo © Llancaiach Fawr Manor*

was quietly engaged in some embroidery. They were seen separately an hour or so apart.

The most frequently seen phantom of Llancaiach Fawr is a small, stout woman in a frilled bonnet and with a bunch of keys hanging from her waist. She is thought to be a former housekeeper and has been nicknamed 'Mattie'. Former occupants as well as visitors have reported sightings of this friendly soul.

Llancaiach is also said to be haunted by two children. They too have friendly dispositions; one indeed became the playfellow of two little girls who lived in the house in the 19th century, without them realising at first that he was not of this earth. The other is also a small boy. He is believed to have died in a tragic accident, having fallen out of a window in the early 1900s. This affectionate spook has been known to follow visitors about the grounds. He has even been reported to have followed them home!

In 2006 Llancaiach Fawr hit the news after the BBC set up a 'ghost cam' in the house. In one frame a small figure can be seen apparently descending the staircase. Could it be one of the ghostly children?

GHOSTS IN THE GROUNDS

The grand mansion of Aberglasney (www.aberglasney.org) stands in Carmarthenshire's beautiful Tywi valley. The current house was built in the late Middle Ages, then greatly remodelled in 1603 and again in 1710, but this is a site of considerable antiquity: until it was sold in the 15th century, this had been the seat of an important local family for ten generations and their original home had probably been a simple wooden longhouse.

The house itself is undergoing restoration but the main attraction for most visitors is the delightful environment of its fabulous gardens, which include a rare survival of an Elizabethan promenade garden. The grounds are said to be haunted by not one but six ghosts, the spirits of maidservants who suffocated one night in a bedroom (either because of a blocked chimney or the presence of freshly applied lead paint, depending on the version you believe). Ghostly phenomena have also been reported within the house but are rather vague. Veteran ghost-hunter Peter Underwood, in his *Ghosts of Wales* (1978, but reprinted as *Haunted Wales* in 2010), states:

'There are those who say they have heard the sound of muffled fighting; those who have heard a mumbled sermon interrupted by the grating of a chair followed by silence; those who have heard the sound of quarrelling and the clink of coins; those who heard a snatch of a wrathful voice denouncing the devil drink;

those who have heard the grumbling voices of discontented tenants . . .'

When Underwood visited Aberglasney he learnt that the church at nearby Llangathen is also haunted. A party of paranormal investigators heard eerie moans and groans in the empty church and also the sound of a door slamming, for which they could not account. They also identified a number of 'cold spots' in the building, where the temperature was considerably, and inexplicably, lower than the surroundings.

SANDS OF TIME

The location of Rhossili Rectory is an extraordinarily lonely one, isolated among a waste of sand dunes on Gower. It's hard to imagine what possessed the Victorian builders to site it here, since it is nowhere near the church or any facilities. It must have been a bleak house indeed to live in and it's no wonder so many ghostly tales have grown up around it. There are rumours of a cold presence that used to visit the house after first emerging from the sea, and of the apparitions of two hideously disfigured people who may have chosen the Rectory to live in simply because it was so far from habitation and prying eyes.

But the best-known ghost is that of one of the Victorian vicars of Rhossili, the Rev John Ponsonby Lucas. He was quite a character by all accounts and enjoyed the isolation, using the broad stretch of beach to exercise his horse, a black stallion. His phantom and that of his beloved steed are still said to be seen galloping along the sands. His is not the only ghost to take a turn along the beach. The wicked Squire Mansell rides in his ghostly coach here, too, searching for treasure. Legend has it he found a large quantity of valuables washed up by the tide, possibly because of ship-wrecking activities, and ever since then his greed knew no bounds, continuing even into the afterlife.

If you fancy a week or two in this famously haunted house, which also happens to be situated in one of the most beautiful parts of Wales (the Gower was the first place in the UK to be designated an Area of Outstanding Natural Beauty), then you'll be delighted to know it is now a holiday home and capable of sleeping up to eleven people.

FRIGHTS AT THE MUSEUM

Museums are repositories not only of historic artefacts but also of memories. It should come as no surprise to learn that so many are believed to be haunted. This is certainly true of Swansea Museum on Oystermouth Road.

In 2010 a local journalist, Richard Thomas, made a particular study of the Swansea Museum ghosts, gleaning interesting paranormal experiences from members of staff. He wrote up his

A repository of memories, Swansea Museum has stirred up a few ghosts. Photo © Richard Thomas

report for *Paranormal Magazine*, a publication I was then editing. Richard learnt that several employees at the museum had glimpsed a 'dark-cloaked figure' on the main staircase. On one occasion witness Catherine Perrie saw it run up a flight of stairs leading to the so-called 'Cabinet of Curiosities', a room which seems to be the focus of the ghostly goings-on.

Cold spots and a 'presence' in the Cabinet of Curiosities gallery have frequently been reported by visitors. Staff member Paul Giuffrida had an eerie experience in this room, too. Working alone on a new exhibition, he was disturbed by 'a lot of noise . . . tapping and banging' coming from a corner of the room even though, aside from himself, it remained unnervingly empty. In the museum's collection centre in the Landore district of Swansea, Mr Giuffrida had another spooky experience: he was disturbed by 'loud whistling' in the apparently empty storage area.

Even the man in charge of Swansea Museum, Roger Gale, has encountered a ghost, although at first he was a little embarrassed to admit this fact to Richard Thomas. Mr Gale saw a ghost walk out of a solid wall and then proceed down a corridor before vanishing. The astonished Mr Gale had the apparition in view for up to twenty seconds. He said it was so lifelike that despite its unorthodox arrival, he initially thought it was one of his colleagues.

THE MONKS OF TINTERN AND NEATH

A celebrated case of alleged communication from beyond the grave took place at Tintern Abbey. It was set down in volume two of *Lord Halifax's Ghost Book* by the husband of the medium who made contact but their names have remained anonymous. In 1895 this man and his wife were on a cycling tour of Monmouthshire and decided to spend the night at Tintern. It was such a glorious evening that they went for a stroll round the romantically moonlit ruins. As they took a rest on a block of masonry, his wife's hand began to twitch. From time to time she had had success at automatic writing, in which spirits are supposed to communicate through the hand of the medium, and

An old drawing of a Cistercian monk, such as those who are said to haunt the ruins of Tintern and Neath abbeys

The romantic ruins of Tintern Abbey were the setting for a famous case of spirit communication.

she recognised the symptoms. She was convinced a spirit was trying to get through. There followed a lengthy period of going through the alphabet with the alleged spirit, the right letter being identified by her hand rapping down on her knee. In this way she was able to build up a story.

The spirit, if such it was, claimed to be a Saxon soldier who had been killed in battle at Tintern. Although he explained that an earlier abbey had existed on the site, he had been buried without

Tintern Abbey

the Last Rites, and he therefore remained restless in the afterlife. The woman agreed to arrange two Masses to be said for the soldier's soul and there the communication ceased. In the end four Masses were said for him by a priest who was a friend of the couple.

In 1905, ten years later, at a séance at the couple's London home, a message came through: 'Very many thanks for the Masses said.' As the message was received through the usual raps, the faint apparition of a bearded man 'dressed in strange close-fitting clothes of a grey material' was seen standing behind the medium.

Although the Saxon soldier has long since departed the scene, a phantom monk has been observed in more recent years at Tintern Abbey. Dressed in a grey habit, he is seen kneeling as though in prayer just beyond an arched doorway.

Phantom monks are also to be encountered at Neath Abbey, which like Tintern was originally built in the 12th century before being abandoned during the Dissolution of the Monasteries during the reign of Henry VIII. Local legend has it that the ghost is of a monk who betrayed the doomed King Edward II to his enemies when he was hiding out in the Abbey in the 1300s. Robert King, author of a recently published book on the *Ghosts of Neath* (Amberley, 2012), has collected several accounts of sightings of this apparition. The monk has been seen in the

A phantom monk – or monks – has been seen in both the grounds and the neighbourhood of Neath Abbey.

main entrance making his way towards a spot where the Abbey church once stood and also in an open area bordering the River Clydach, the site of the medieval burial ground.

A ghostly monk – he may not of course be the same ghost – has also been reported crossing a nearby hump-backed bridge over the canal. On this occasion his face was observable: described as 'pleasant enough' by the witness and belonging to a man in his thirties or forties. The odd thing about this sighting, though, is that the bridge was constructed in the 19th century, at least four hundred years after the last monks had left Neath.

MYSTERIOUS MONUMENTS

Wales is rich in ancient monuments, including hundreds of enigmatic standing stones. Some of these monoliths are prehistoric; others are the stumps of early Christian preaching crosses or pre-Christian monuments that were 'Christianised' in the Dark Ages by scratching crosses onto them. Several standing stones have ghost stories attached to them.

Bodvoc Stone

One of the most interesting standing stones in Wales has now found a home, along with many others, in the Margam Stones Museum in Neath Port Talbot. It's known as the 'Bodvoc Stone' because this is the name that is boldly scratched on its surface. Bodvoc's identity is lost in the mists of time but he was presumably some worthy of the Dark Ages, when the stone was set up.

According to local legend, Bodvoc haunted the stone commemorating him and guarded a treasure that was buried beneath it. Fear of the ghost failed to outweigh greed for the imagined gold, however, and this important monument was so undermined by would-be treasure-hunters that it fell over.

Eventually it was taken down from the mountain above the village of Margam where it had stood for centuries and placed for safety in the museum.

Sagranus Stone

This is another Dark Age monument known after the name engraved upon it. The memorial to the mysterious 'Sagranus' dates from the 6th century and is in both Latin and Ogham, an ancient alphabet which takes the form of chiselled cuts. The discovery of the Sagranus Stone helped scholars translate Ogham for the first time.

It is something of a miracle that both the stone and its inscriptions survived because for many years it was used as a bridge over a stream – fortunately with the inscribed side facing down. During the day it had plenty of use, so the writing would certainly have been worn down to nothing if it had been placed the other way up. At night, oddly enough, it tended not be used; indeed the villagers preferred to avoid it after dark. This is because at midnight it was used by a ghost – another example of the ubiquitous White Lady – as she wandered round the countryside.

The Sagranus Stone is now safely on display in the parish church of St Dogmael's (Llandudoch), near where it was found on the Pembrokeshire–Ceredigion border.

One of the Bronze Age standing stones which line a field called Parc y Marw, or 'Field of the Dead', which was considered so badly haunted that people would avoid it after dark.

Parc y Marw

Another Pembrokeshire ancient site is also haunted by a White Lady. Near the village of Llanychaer a line of standing stones dating from the Bronze Age can still be seen bordering a field with the suggestive name of Parc y Marw (or 'Field of the Dead'). The White Lady haunting Parc y Marw must have been particularly scary because the public footpath diverts a mile out of its way to avoid the field. Victorian antiquarians studying the stones learnt that the locals were keen to keep clear of Parc y Marw at night in case they encountered the ghost.

Goat's Hole

Making a change from White Ladies, we can now consider a 'Red Lady'. The 'Red Lady of Paviland' is a skeleton found in 1823 in Goat's Hole, one of the Paviland Caves on the Gower coast. It earned its name from the fact that the bones had been coloured using a red dye as some kind of funeral rite. Dating from more than 30,000 years ago, the skeleton is the oldest example in Britain of human remains displaying a ceremonial burial practice.

For many years Goat's Hole had a reputation of being haunted. It is a tidal cave which becomes flooded by the sea, and the story behind the supposed ghost was that a woman had one day got trapped in the cave and drowned at high tide. The discovery of the so-called 'Red Lady' confirmed the legend in the minds of the local populace, despite the skeleton's great antiquity and the fact that it was soon identified as having belonged to a man! Of course, these contrary details don't necessarily scotch the possibility of Goat's Hole being haunted, just the story behind it. The ghost may even be that of the prehistoric man who was laid to rest so reverently in the dark depths of the cave those many thousands of years ago.

HAUNTED HOSTELRIES

There are so many haunted pubs and inns in Britain that numerous books have been devoted to them. If one believes in ghosts as the returning spirits of the dead, this is perhaps not so surprising. Many pubs have been the hub of their communities for centuries and thousands of souls will have spent a sizeable proportion of their lives in them. Perhaps restless spirits seek out the places where in life they have been happiest or felt they most belonged. In this chapter there follows a brief selection of some of the region's many haunted pubs and hotels.

Skirrid Mountain Inn

In 1978, when ghost-hunter Peter Underwood visited the Skirrid Mountain Inn in Monmouthshire, he noted that it was 'supposed to be haunted' and that the ghost 'was a friendly one', although it was a vague presence at best and its identity was a mystery. Twenty years later, when Roy Palmer published his *The Folklore of (Old) Monmouthshire* in 1998, he also recorded just one ghost at the Skirrid Inn, that of a one-eyed man who had stabbed himself rather than suffer at the hands of the infamous

'Hanging' Judge Jeffreys. Jeffreys is said to have used the hostelry as a makeshift courtroom after the Monmouth Rebellion in 1685.

Over the subsequent fifteen years the haunted reputation of the Skirrid Inn has grown and grown, thanks to numerous private and commercial ghost-hunting events, including several broadcast on TV. It is now promoted as the most haunted public house in Wales. Among the newly discovered ghosts is the spirit of a former landlady called Fanny Price who makes herself known in a variety of ways, not all of them subtle (she enjoys chucking glasses about, for example). Some people have also claimed to have experienced a disturbing phenomenon which presumably dates back to the dark days of the Hanging Judge: the feeling that a noose is being slipped around their neck. In response to this a landlord with a black sense of humour has now dangled a noose down the depth of the stairwell as a grisly ornament.

Queen's Head Hotel

This handsome half-timbered building in James Street, Monmouth, is now a community pub and prides itself on its welcoming atmosphere. It offers live music, log fires and a free lending library among its attractions. This venerable hotel was formerly a favourite of Oliver Cromwell. During the Civil War a Cavalier made an attempt on his life while he was staying here, and the bullet holes can still be seen in the rafters. The assassination was unsuccessful, of course, and the Royalist was chased into the bar and shot. His sad ghost is said to be seen hovering near the fireplace in the bar, this presumably being the spot where he was killed.

A ghostly male figure has also been reported wandering up and down an upstairs landing. It is tempting to think this may be the same ghost seen making his stealthy approach to Cromwell's former bedroom. Although described as 'shadowy and vague', it is nevertheless considered to be an entirely different spook. Finally there is the apparition of a little girl who has been seen in various parts of the hotel.

Duke of Wellington

The mysterious entity haunting the Duke of Wellington in Old Market Street, Neath, is a ghost with attitude and has been known to get violent. For reasons seemingly now forgotten, the spook has been nicknamed 'the Captain' and is rarely seen, although he did make one notable exception in 1993 when he turned up as a man-sized shape on a video recording which was then broadcast UK-wide on a daytime TV show.

Neath historian Robert King has learnt of two remarkable incidents involving the Captain. The Duke of Wellington is a popular live music venue but one night the ghost apparently objected to the noise, or at least to a local band's singer, because the microphone stand suddenly reared up and struck him a blow on the head. The startled singer and audience then watched in amazement as the metal stand neatly replaced itself. Rather more serious was the occasion when a young man at the bar, on hearing that the pub was allegedly haunted, scoffed at the very idea of ghosts. Shortly afterwards he made a visit to the gents and then hurriedly returned, his face bleeding. Something invisible had lashed out at him.

'Something hit me, but there was nothing in the toilet,' he said. 'Something just bashed me in the face. It hit me twice. There was no sound.'

One can only assume the unfortunate young man is not so sceptical now.

Castle Hotel

In his fascinating book, *Ghosts of Neath* (2012), Robert King details the hauntings of a number of other pubs in Neath, including its largest, the historic Castle Hotel. The apparition of a bearded man in dark clothes picked out with bright silver buttons has been seen in the bar by several members of staff over the years. His identity is a mystery.

Equally mysterious is the barking of a dog that has been heard at night echoing up from the deep cellars. The baying, which has been described as being 'both mournful and aggressive', emanates from behind a bricked-up archway. The current owners have no intention of demolishing the bricks to find out what lies behind them, however. That might be seen as an invitation to the phantom hound for it to climb the stairs and bark at the guests!

Pontardawe Inn

This interesting old inn is situated in a little village tucked away in a valley near Swansea. Two drovers' routes cross at Pontardawe and there has probably been an inn here for many centuries. Nearby there is a most unusual feature, an engraving of a witch scratched under the arch of the bridge (or 'pont' in Welsh) over the River Dawe. The bridge was constructed in the 18th century but no one knows when the carving was made, nor why – but it certainly hints at mysterious forces at work in this deep, secluded valley.

Spooky goings-on are commonplace in the Pontardawe Inn and on the whole they are typical of those reported by staff at other haunted pubs around the UK. For example, the rumble of beer kegs being moved about in the cellar has not infrequently been heard, even though the cellar is empty at the time and the kegs are always undisturbed.

Pub ghosts are attracted to glasses, too. The Pontardawe spook likes to hurl glasses from the shelves so that they land with some force on the stone flags of the bar. However, they do not smash as they should: instead they are made to spin round and round before rattling to a halt. Staff learnt from a visitor who had stayed in the pub during the Second World War that the mischievous presence also enjoyed scattering the sticks she had carefully laid in the fire grate all over the floor by the time she had returned with the coal.

In 2008 the South Wales Paranormal Research group learnt from the landlord that on just one occasion an apparition was seen in the pub, possibly the entity that has been causing all the trouble. He described it as 'a white figure, approximately the height of a small child'. He had looked up from some work he was engaged in to see it apparently watching him. On his looking up, however, it immediately made its exit, by walking straight through the table he was sitting at and then vanishing through the wall.

Rhymney House Hotel

Originally built as a private home in 1801, this charming family-friendly hotel boasts splendid views of the lovely Rhymney Valley. According to the South Wales Paranormal Research group it also boasts numerous ghosts, including 'a lady in a white mob cap and dress, a young child, an old lady by the fire, a black shadowy figure and a dominant male with a rod'. Inexplicable noises have also been reported.

When another ghost-hunting group, the Ghostknights, carried out an investigation here some years ago, they heard mysterious footsteps, the miaowing of an invisible cat and a door making a loud slamming noise even though it was already closed. They also glimpsed a menacing shadow apparently crouching at the top of a flight of stairs and saw a 'cream-coloured' apparition, possibly of a child, make its way from a bathroom and into a bedroom where three people watched it as it disappeared through what is now an external wall.

Craig y Nos Castle

Craig y Nos Castle is a splendid Victorian mansion which was designed to suit the Alpine-like scenery of the Upper Swansea

Ghostly goings-on have frequently been reported from the grand Victorian mansion that is now the Craig y Nos Castle Hotel.
Photo © Wayne Davies Aerial Photography for Craig y Nos Castle

Valley (Craig y Nos means 'Crag of the Night'). Built by a Captain Rice Davies Powell in the 1840s, the Castle (which is not really a castle, of course) was sold in 1876 to Adelina Patti, a celebrated opera singer.

An Italian by birth, Adelina Patti found great fame in Britain and even performed at private parties hosted by Queen Victoria. She settled in Britain so as to be close to her adoring fans but looked out for a house where she could get away from them when she wanted to. Craig y Nos suited her perfectly – or rather it did so once she had added two wings, a clock tower, a conservatory and a private theatre. A very wealthy woman, Patti lavished money on the mansion: it became the first private home in Wales to be fitted with electric lighting.

Although she was married, Patti's husband did not join her at Craig y Nos. Instead she moved in with her favourite tenor, Ernesto Nicolini. It says something for both her fame and her personality that such behaviour was overlooked in Victorian Britain.

Adelina Patti loved Craig y Nos so much that her spirit, it is claimed, has never really left it. The Castle is now a hotel and staff and guests alike have reported her gentle presence throughout her former home. One account tells of a guest who visited the private theatre and sat for a while at the piano, tapping out a few notes. Suddenly she found herself playing that sentimental old ditty *Home Sweet Home*. It was not a tune she had

The private theatre at Craig y Nos Castle Hotel was specially constructed for former owner Adelina Patti, whose benign presence is believed to still haunt the room. Photo © Craig y Nos Castle

played before and she would have been unable to play it through ordinarily without the sheet music in front of her. This odd experience took on an eerie aspect when the lady learnt that *Home Sweet Home* was a song Adelina Patti had made famous.

Room 36 in the hotel is considered particularly haunted but apparently by someone other than the famous opera star. Ghost-hunter Richard Felix spent an unquiet night in this room. He said he glimpsed a shadow moving through the wall where, he was subsequently told, a door had once been situated, and he also saw a dark figure lying prone on his own bed!

TOM THE LORD

Once upon a time the charming village of Redwick near Newport was haunted by a spirited – in more ways than one – ghost who was nicknamed 'Tom the Lord'. In life the ghost had been the lord of the manor, a typical country squire of past centuries who enjoyed a drink or two. Not for Tom fine wines or brandy: his favourite tipple was the scrumpy brewed by one of his tenants, Farmer Thorn. Of an evening, he'd make himself comfortable in front of Farmer Thorn's fireside and quaff several pints of his strongest cider. Alas, one fateful night, the squire was staggering home more than usually drunk when he stumbled into a ditch, passed out and drowned.

However, Farmer Thorn's cider was so good that it enticed the boozy spirit of Tom the Lord back from beyond the grave. Soon after the squire had been apparently laid to his rest, Farmer Thorn opened up his barn in the morning to find the taps on his barrels had been opened and a goodly quantity of the scrumpy was missing. This state of affairs went on for some time, with the puzzled farmer unable to catch the thief no matter what he did – and no wonder!

After a while, the true nature – or rather supernature – of the scrumpy scrumper became known, when Tom the Lord's ghost became visible. He also became more troublesome. He would take to visiting the village as well as the farm, and the people of Redwick began to stay firmly behind closed doors after

The Rose Inn at Redwick. A drunken ghost called 'Tom the Lord' made a nuisance of himself in Redwick for many years.

sundown. The ghost's favourite haunt was a hedge opposite Rose Cottage, where he'd sit and regard his former estate. His unearthly presence made the hedge wither and die. The canny Farmer Thorn made a kind of bargain with Tom the Lord: he constructed a stile in the hedge for the ghost to sit on and every evening he would leave a mug of cider there for him to drink. In this way, he was able to stop the raids on his cider barrels.

This could only ever be a temporary solution, however. The villagers were fed up with having a drunken ghost hanging about the place so they brought in not one but twelve ministers to carry out an exorcism. Even they had a tough time convincing Tom the Lord to give up the cider and turn instead to the Other Side.

WICKED JUAN WHITE

According to legend, the mountains of South Wales were haunted by the ghost of a witch. In life she was Juan White and lived in a cottage near Pontypool. After her death she took to haunting the high, misty hills above Ebbw Vale and the Rhondda. Back in the days before metalled roads and motorised transport, people in rural areas were used to walking miles to work or market, and in Wales in particular this might take them across wild and empty uplands where they would trudge their solitary way for hours without seeing another person, having to rely on their knowledge of the area or their wits to avoid bogs and precipices.

For this reason wicked Juan White would delight in haunting the mountains in search of lonely travellers whom she would then attempt to lead astray, preferably to their doom over a cliff. If she couldn't manage that, she'd do her best to get them stuck in a bog or simply encourage them to go miles out of their way, where they would become lost and benighted on the mountain.

An evil spirit known as Juan White would take the form of an innocent-looking old woman and then lead people dangerously astray on South Wales's wildest mountains. The illustration is by T H Thomas and taken from British Goblins, published in 1880.

This was quite an easy job for the ghostly witch. Solitary travellers would be so grateful at the sight of a fellow human being in those bleak expanses that they would tend to follow any distant figure, assuming they knew the way.

To further encourage people to follow her, Juan White would dress like an old lady carrying a milk-can. Walkers would naturally assume an old lady couldn't walk far and that an easy route down couldn't be far away. The milk-can also suggested she was on a short journey to or from her cows or a neighbour's house. However, the traveller could never get close enough to join her or ask the way – the ghost would keep just too far ahead of them, never apparently increasing her pace but somehow staying the same distance apart even if the other person ran to catch up. By the time they'd realised something weird was going on, it would usually be too late: they'd find themselves surrounded by marsh or in an unfamiliar and treacherous part of the mountain, with cliffs and crevasses on all sides. This trick worked best when mists and drizzle had descended on the mountains, reducing visibility.

Once she had achieved her wicked purpose, the spectral witch would like as not stand and laugh at the unfortunate traveller. When she wasn't wandering about the mountains searching for victims on foot, Juan would trundle about in a phantom coach. It was rarely seen but could be heard rattling through the passes and up narrow sheep tracks where it would be impossible for any real coach to go. She would also call out a cry of 'Wow-up!' which might be heard echoing off the rocks and peaks. 'Wow-up!' was a recognised call in South Wales, a kind of SOS for people injured or lost on a mountain. In this way, Juan would also lure people on, because they believed there was some poor soul in need of aid.

HOUNDS THAT HAUNT

One of the most enduring characters in British folklore is the Black Dog. These are pretty much what-it-says-on-the-tin spooks: they take the form of dog-like creatures, normally black in colour, and they tended to haunt lonely lanes and byways. They weren't always black, they were often more cow- or donkey-like than dog-like but they were generally huge in size, much bigger than any breed of dog.

They've been encountered in quite recent times. In England they went by various regional names, such as Padfoot, Trash and Skriker. In Wales they were known as Gwyllgi, an obscure word which probably translates as 'Dogs of the Twilight' in old Welsh. Twilight was certainly the time when they were most often seen.

At Skewen, Neath Port Talbot, one of these phantom animals followed home a farmer's girl late one night. She said it caught up with her and then literally dogged her footsteps all the way to her door – typical Gwyllgi behaviour. She, no doubt, was in

Sherlock Holmes and Dr Watson encounter 'The Hound of the Baskervilles'
in this illustration to Conan Doyle's celebrated novel published in 1902.
Doyle based his story on the ghostly Black Dogs reported from all over
Britain, including South Wales.

*A lane connecting the castle of Laugharne with the village was formerly
haunted by a spectral hound which used to set up
a terrifying howl.*

an agony of suspense as to what it might do. She believed it was
'the devil'. When she got back to the farm, her employer
grabbed his gun and went out into the night in search of the
creature. He saw nothing, but the next morning weird footprints
were found in the muddy lane. From that day the track was
known as Llwybr y Cythraul, or The Devil's Pathway.

Another Gwyllgi was encountered by a man named Davies in a lane leading to Newchurch, Carmarthenshire. It 'grinned terribly' at him but Mr Davies refused to be intimidated by the scary critter: he took a swipe at it with his walking stick. The stick went right through the spook and struck the ground. The disconcerted Gwyllgi vanished and Mr Davies was able to continue on his way without any further ado.

A similar beast haunted another Carmarthenshire village, Laugharne. A young woman named Rebecca Adam came across it on a lane connecting the village with the castle. Unusually for Welsh Black Dogs, which tended to be silent, this one liked to howl. Some examples from England were very noisy; indeed the name Skriker comes from the archaic verb 'to skrike' meaning to scream or make a fuss. Poor Rebecca must have been alarmed enough at finding a huge ghostly animal barring her way: imagine how she felt when the Gwyllgi then sat down and, according to her tale, 'set up such a scream, so horrible, so loud, and so strong, that she thought the earth moved under her'.

These mysterious apparitions were being seen well into the 20th century. A Mr Phillips saw one on two separate occasions on the road between Haverfordwest (Hwlffordd) and Pembroke Dock (Doc Penfro). In 1920 he wrote a letter about it to the national archaeology magazine of Wales, *Archaeologia Cambrensis* (I'm guessing Mr Phillips was himself an archaeologist). He said this Gwyllgi was black in colour, similar in size to a St Bernard, but its forequarters were more like those of a goat or a calf than a dog and it had short horns. On one of the occasions on which he saw it he was only a few yards away and the night was brightly lit by the moon, so he was able to see it clearly. One wonders whether these strange spectres are the ghosts of prehistoric animals long since extinct. However, this supposition wouldn't explain the oddest aspects of some of these spooks, including the really weird one seen near Llysworney in the Vale of Glamorgan.

This one was encountered late one night by a man named Anthony. It appeared in a hollow lane leading to Crossways, the farm where he worked. Its body was dog-like, though spotted or piebald rather than the more usual black, but its head was horribly human in appearance and it had 'bright, moonlike eyes'. Welshmen of the 19th century certainly had some guts because Anthony showed the same spirit when confronted by this terrifying apparition as had Mr Davies, mentioned above. Unlike Mr Davies, he had no walking stick to fend it off with. All he had was a hat, so he waved that in the monster's face. This was enough to dispel the ghostly presence and it disappeared. I guess there is a lesson to be learnt from this: no matter how scary the ghost, it can no more harm you physically than an average Welsh spider can.

We'll encounter one more strange, dog-like ghost in the following chapter.

GHOSTS UNDERGROUND

Throughout history miners have been recognised as being particularly superstitious; and no wonder, working in the dark all day or night in perilous conditions. This was certainly true of the Welsh colliers. A researcher by the name of Martin Phillips gathered a considerable amount of ghostly folklore from a vast coal mine, the Morfa Pit at Port Talbot.

The Morfa Pit was more than usually prone to explosions of gas and rock falls. The heightened tension of this dangerous environment led to a belief in numerous apparitions, all of which the colliers believed manifested when an accident was about to occur. Sometimes they took the form of odd lights or noises (perhaps genuine geological phenomena), and even a paranormal aroma, said to waft from an invisible 'death flower'. Far more dramatic were the phantom trams which were seen 'running wild in the pit'. These were said to be drawn by a deathly white horse. Also reported was 'a strange man in oilskins' who would suddenly appear in the cage or on a train of trams to the terror of the miners. The ghostly horse was not the only phantom animal associated with the mine. A great white bird was seen the day before an explosion in which 89 men and boys were killed. The flapping of an invisible bird was also considered an omen (this is known as the Aderyn Cyrff or Corpse Bird in Wales). Rats infested the pit and they too had significance in the miners' superstitions. The sudden disappearance of rats from an area of the mine was a clue that deadly gas such as 'firedamp' was about. However, there was less logic in the belief in a huge white rat, the sighting of which was a warning of impending danger.

Perhaps the strangest of all the phantom animals believed to haunt the colliery was The Red Dog of Morfa. We have already met with spooky Black Dogs in this book, but this is the only one described as being blood red in colour. Of course, a Black Dog in a coal mine would have been all but invisible so maybe this explains the colour change!

THE GLOOMIEST GHOSTS OF ALL

The various paranormal phenomena reported from the Morfa Colliery are all examples of ghostly omens, warnings of coming danger or death. In Wales such phenomena were known under the label of 'Tolaeth', a word of obscure origin that may possibly have its root in the Welsh word for family, 'teulu', since such spooks usually involved family members.

Although supernatural death omens are known in the folklore of all areas of the British Isles, there are far more reports about them in Wales than anywhere else. In the past, the Tolaeth seem to have formed a national obsession. According to legend, it was the patron saint of Wales, St David, who brought about the existence of the Tolaeth. According to an 18th-century writer: 'Being a very spiritual man, and living under a sense of eternity after this short life, as all very spiritual men do, and observing that the people in general were careless of the life to come, and could not be brought to mind it, and make a preparation for it, though he laboured much to bring them to it, he prayed God to give a sign of the immortality of the soul, and of a life to come, a presage of death and motive to prepare for it; and that God, in answer to his prayer, sent the corpse-candles and likely the Kyhirraeth, to answer the same pious end. This is the tradition of the country about it.'

The Tolaeth took many forms, including the Corpse Candles and the banshee-like Cyhiraeth (modern spelling) mentioned above.

Corpse Candles

Corpse Candles or, more properly, Canwyllau Cyrff, were small lights which would be seen either hovering near a person who would shortly die or which would be seen travelling at night from the home of the doomed person to the local graveyard, following the route that would be later taken by the funeral procession. They could be more elaborate, appearing as candles being carried by the shade of the person due to die, or as candles within skulls.

An early 19th-century engraving of a Corpse Candle, or Canwyll Cyrff, a mysterious ball of light the sighting of which would warn of a coming death.

One author, James Motley, encountered what he believed to be Corpse Candles and wrote about the experience in his 1848 book *Tales of the Cymry*: 'In many instances, [the Corpse Candles] seem to be of electrical origin, when the ears of the traveller's horse, the extremity of his whip, his spurs, or any other projecting points appear tipped with pencils of light. The writer was once witness to this in a very extraordinary degree, during cold weather in the month of January, 1842, on the mountain road from Maesteg to Aberafon: upon this occasion, the toes of the rider's boots, and even the tufts of hair at the fetlocks of his horse, appeared to burn with a steady blue light, and on the hand being extended, every finger immediately became tipped with fire.'

A couple of interesting accounts of Corpse Candles come from Llandeilo, Carmarthenshire. One was seen by a man named Joshua Coslet at a place called Heol Bwlch y Wynt (Wind Gap Lane). He described it as a small light which grew bigger the further away from him it went. He also saw 'that there was some dark shadow passing along with the Candle; but he was afraid to look earnestly upon it'. This shadow was probably that of the unfortunate person doomed to die. It was only a short time after Joshua's sighting that a burial passed through Wind Gap Lane.

Three men crossing the river south of Llandeilo died when their coracle overturned. A day or two before this tragedy, the passengers on a coach which ran between Llandeilo and Carmarthen had seen three Corpse Candles floating on the water precisely where these men lost their lives. There was a fourth man with the doomed trio, but at the last minute he decided not to risk the crossing when he saw how dangerously the river was in flood. He had known nothing about the death omens which had previously been seen.

A particularly striking example of a Canwyll Cyrff was seen at Taf Fechan Chapel in Neuadd parish, near Builth Wells. Walter Watkins and his mother and father watched the pulsing light as it repeatedly increased and decreased in size, first appearing as small as a star, then growing until it was 'as big as a Church Tower'. Some time later a neighbour was ploughing in a field near the chapel, in about the position where the Canwyll Cyrff was seen, and he uncovered an anonymous grave. Inside it was an earthen jug and the jawbone of a man.

The description suggests this may have been a prehistoric burial, but the rumour-mill started and it was soon decided they were in fact the remains of a man who had disappeared some years previously. When his wife, who had since remarried, was told – as a bad joke – that her husband had returned, the poor woman fell ill with the shock and shortly afterwards died.

Phantom funerals

Another commonly reported example of the Tolaeth, these were apparitions of funeral processions that were shortly to take place in the parish. They would either be seen making their sombre way at twilight through the lanes to the local graveyard, or they would be invisible, but the sounds of the shuffling feet, sobbing or hymn-singing of the mourners would be heard. Rarely would a phantom funeral be both seen and heard.

Once upon a time people living in South Wales who found themselves walking after sundown would always keep close to the edge of the road just in case they accidentally came into contact with an invisible phantom funeral. They could be quite dangerous, as the following story from a village near Tenby in Pembrokeshire demonstrates.

The manservant of the Rector of Penally was in love with a pretty servant girl at Holloway Farm, and used to steal out at night to visit her. These meetings were heartily disapproved of by the Rector. One November evening, coming home, this romantic fellow was passing the turn of the road which led from Holloway to Penally, when he saw a silent funeral procession approaching him. He pressed himself into the hedge to let the people pass by, but the mourners – some of whom he recognised – 'jostled so rudely against him, that they hurt and bruised him severely, not heeding his entreaties or cries'. At last, free of the brutal treatment he received from the phantoms, he watched the procession continue on a strange course: it went over a hedge into the next field, then made a detour, before returning over the same hedge further on.

The next morning, he awoke bruised and sore and begged his master to give him a day off. The Rector refused to believe his servant's tale, however, and accused him of having been 'drinking and fighting' in an alehouse! Some weeks later an incident occurred to prove the man's story was true. Heavy snow had fallen and the weather was bitterly cold. The Holloway farmer died, and many followed his procession to Penally churchyard. The great snowdrifts confused the bearers, however,

A dramatic account of a phantom funeral – the ghost of a funeral that will shortly come to pass – has been reported from the pretty village of Penally, near Tenby in Pembrokeshire.

and they missed the road under its featureless white blanket, passing by mistake into the next field. They processed a little way through the field, the mourners following, until, realising their mistake, they came back onto the road, by the very same detour the manservant had witnessed three weeks previously.

Elsewhere in Pembrokeshire, in the Gwaun Valley between Fishguard and Pontfaen, a young man encountered a phantom funeral in 1905. He told his story to the folklorist J C Davies a few years after it happened. He explained to Davies that he had been sitting by the bedside of a friend who was dying and was therefore up very late. Davies continues:

'About three o'clock in the morning the patient was so seriously ill that my informant in alarm hurried to call the father of the poor sufferer to come to see him, as the old man lived in a small cottage close by. As soon as he went out through the door into the open air, to his great astonishment he found himself in a large crowd of people, and there was a coffin resting on some chairs, ready to be placed on the bier; and the whole scene, as it were, presented a funeral procession, ready to convey the dead to the grave.

'When the young man attempted to proceed on his way, the procession also proceeded, or moved on in the same direction so that he found himself still in the crowd. After going on in this manner for about a hundred yards, he managed to draw [to] one side from the crowd and soon reached the house of his sick friend's father, and nearly fainted.

'Three days after this vision the seer's friend died; and on the day of the funeral the young man noticed that the crowd stood in front of the house and the coffin resting on chairs exactly as he had seen in the apparition. I may add that my informant who had seen the phantom funeral was so terrified even at the time when I saw him, that he was too much afraid to go out at night.'

Unearthly sounds

Inexplicable knocks, taps, bangs and groans might be heard in a house where someone was dying or a death was to occur. Many carpenters reported hearing the sounds of a coffin being made in their workshops at night, only to receive an order for a coffin the following morning.

An interesting and detailed account of weird noises afflicting a house comes from Newcastle Emlyn (Castell Newydd Emlyn) on the borders of Carmarthenshire, Pembrokeshire and Ceredigion. The incidents took place in the years 1882 and 1883 in the home of a tailor, Samuel Thomas, and his wife. It is another story collected by the folklorist J C Davies, who in his book *Folk-Lore of West and Mid-Wales* (1911) explains:

'One morning, very early, Thomas heard a knocking at the door of his bedroom, and he enquired from his bed "Who is there?" but there was no reply. The next morning he heard knocking at the front door. He exclaimed from his bed: "All right, I am getting up now." But when he did get up and opened the door, not a single soul could be seen anywhere. Thomas was perplexed as to who could have come to disturb him at five o'clock in the morning, two mornings one after the other, and disappear so mysteriously. No voice had been heard, nor the sound of footsteps, only a knocking at the door.

'Twelve months to the very day after this a brother of Thomas came to spend a day with him. This was in the first week of

January, 1883. In the evening Thomas went to his workshop, and when he was busily engaged in making a suit of clothes, he heard a knocking at the window quite suddenly – two knocks. He thought that some friend outside wanted to call his attention to something; but when he looked at the window there was no one to be seen. After a while the knocking went on again, and continued for about ten minutes.

'The next night the knocking at the window continued as it had on the previous evening, but nothing was to be seen. On the third night there was a knocking at the window several times, and it was much louder or more violent than it had been on the two previous evenings. The tailor and his young assistant now decided to keep their eyes on the window, and as soon as they did so there was no more knocking; but the moment they ceased looking and resumed their work, the knocking was heard again. There were several young men in the room that evening and they heard the knocking, and even his wife heard it from another part of the house.

'These "spirit knockings" had now been noised abroad everywhere, and amongst others who went there to hear them was the farmer on whose land the tailor lived. The farmer did not believe in superstition, but when he heard the knocking, he was convinced there was something supernatural about it.

'On the fifth night a very loud knock at the door was heard as if someone had attempted to break through. On the sixth evening, when Thomas went out for a short walk, he heard such noise as if two hundred horses were rushing by him. On the seventh and eighth evenings the knocking still continued, and on the ninth, Thomas went out with a gun, and found that there was no one to be seen, but heard some groaning voice in the air and doleful wailing. He returned to the house quite frightened. There was no more knocking after the ninth evening.

'At the beginning of January, 1883, at the same time that these strange knockings and wailings were heard, a woman whose old home had been that of the tailor lay dying in America. One Mr Lloyd, from Newcastle Emlyn, happened to be at her death-bed in America when she was longing in vain to die in her old home in Wales. When she found she was too ill to return, to die at her old home and to be buried alongside her husband who had died before she had left for America, her crying on her death-bed in that far-off land was heart-rending.

'This solves the mystery of the "spirit knockings", and it also confirms the truth of the old belief that Death makes his presence known by knocking at the door of the relatives of friends of those he is about to strike.'

The Cyhiraeth and the Gwrach y Rhibyn

The Cyhiraeth is an invisible spirit that visits houses or entire villages to warn of a death or some other calamity such as an outbreak of disease. Its eerie wailing makes it the Welsh equivalent of the Irish banshee.

According to Charles Redwood, writing in Glamorganshire in the early 19th century, the wailing would 'rise and fall', fading away before suddenly shrieking with 'a fearful loudness . . .

An early 19th-century engraving of the banshee, a weird woman whose mournful cries would warn of a coming death. A banshee wailed outside the place where an Irishman, working in South Wales, lay dying. The banshee has her Welsh equivalent, the Gwrach y Rhibyn.

terrific and unearthly.' He added: 'Sometimes as it [the Cyhiraeth] goes by, something seems to flap against the cottage windows, or the window, maybe, will shake and tremble, the door fly open, and the whole house be filled with horror. And this generally occurs to almost every house on the road-side along which the Cyhiraeth passes.' Another writer described it as sounding like 'a smothered shriek, or a rushing noise resembling the whirring of birds' wings, or a flight of starlings.'

A Mr and Mrs Hall, who took a tour of the region in 1860, heard a tale of a genuine Irish banshee that visited a farm in South Wales while itinerant Irish haymakers were working on it one summer. An elderly Irishman named Martin Blane had become so feeble during the labour that he asked the gentleman farmer if he could rest in his barn, to gather some strength before returning to his native land. The farmer assented and Blane stayed in the barn for some weeks, but he grew weaker rather than stronger.

One night the farmer, whose room faced the barn, 'was startled by a clapping of hands, followed immediately by a wail so loud and unearthly, that he shivered as if with ague'. The apparition he saw which accompanied this wail was 'a female form shrouded from head to foot in a cloak, crouching by the door, sobbing piteously; while ever and anon she repeated the loud cry the farmer had first heard, extending her emaciated arms, and clapping her hands with a fleshless, hard, "bony" sound.'

This went on for some time, the farmer 'paralysed' by the sight and sound of the banshee. Then: 'Suddenly the dark form arose – it was very tall and awful – folded its cloak around it close – close as a bat its wings, crying still, but faintly. After it had faded away in the darkness, he heard the wail, now creeping along the earth, then rising into the sky: he listened breathlessly, but at last it was gone – quite gone.' The farmer hurried over to the barn and there found Martin Blane was dead and all his other servants were 'crouched in one heap at his door'.

In its appearance this banshee resembles another weird Welsh spirit, the Gwrach y Rhibyn. 'Rhibyn' is hard to translate: it refers to the dank, drizzly mist which is all too often encountered on Welsh mountains. One translation I've seen of Gwrach y Rhibyn is 'Hag of the Mountain Dribble'! Like the Cyhiraeth, this eerie spirit wails and cries; but unlike the Cyhiraeth, which is invisible, the Gwrach has a distinct and rather horrible appearance, not dissimilar to that of the banshee described above.

According to Glamorganshire folklorist Marie Trevelyan: 'This spectral form is described as having long black hair, black eyes, and a swarthy countenance. Sometimes one of her eyes is grey and the other black. Both are deeply sunk and piercing. Her back was crooked, her figure was very thin and spare, and her pigeon-breasted bust was concealed by a sombre scarf. Her trailing robes were black. She was sometimes seen with long flapping wings that fell heavily at her sides, and occasionally flying low down along watercourses, or around hoary mansions. Frequently the flapping of her leathern bat-like wings could be heard against the window-panes.'

One of her haunts was a patch of marshy bog below Caerphilly Castle. Another was Pennard Castle, near Swansea. One man foolish enough to sleep in the ruins of Pennard Castle one night encountered the Gwrach y Rhibyn, who attacked him with her talon-like fingernails. He was badly gashed and scratched by the angry spirit and left in a very sorry state, his clothes ripped to shreds.

Ghosts of the living

Not all apparitions are of people who have 'passed on'. There are a surprising number of accounts of ghosts of living people. In some parts of England such a spook was called a 'fetch' and was generally considered a death omen. In Wales the word Lledrith was sometimes used for a ghostly doppelganger.

A young woman was returning to Llanybri, near the Taf estuary, one bright, moonlit night when she was astonished to come across a well-known character in the neighbourhood, an old lady named Rachel y Gweydd (the Weaver), sitting by the roadside, where she was 'busily engaged in knitting a stocking'. When the witness told her mother of what she had seen, that good woman replied; 'Ach y fi, something strange is sure to take place after

Pennard Castle was one of the haunts of the horrifying entity known as the Gwrach y Rhibyn.

this.' And she was right, for a few days later a man named Thomas Davies died and was buried at the Capel Newydd, and there, sitting by the roadside in the very spot where she had been seen in the moonlight, was Rachel the Weaver, knitting a sock and watching the funeral procession go by!

Another strange tale comes from the hills between Brecon and Hay, where a young man caught sight of his wife in that lonely place, beckoning from a cherry tree. He went to find out what she was doing there – but she ran off into the road. He ran after her but try as he might he could not catch up with her. He vainly pursued the energetic lady 'for a mile and a half up hill and down dale', until, finally running out of breath, he was forced to give up the chase. Assuming the performance was all 'done for a frolic', he staggered home, and there found his wife calmly knitting.

'How did you get back?' he asked.

'Get back? Why I've never been anywhere!' she replied. 'I have not been outside the doors since you went to the barn after tea.' In this instance, as in so many where doubles of living people are seen, neither injury nor death followed the sighting. It remained simply one of those meaningless, inexplicable occurrences which so fascinate students of the supernatural.

The mysterious cloud

I shall end on a unique account of a death warning and among the strangest of a very strange set of tales. It took place somewhere within the boundaries of Mynyddislwyn, an old parish now largely incorporated into Caerphilly, and was recorded by a collector of supernatural stories from the 18th century, Edmund Jones.

One day a man named John Elias Jones was ploughing a field when he saw a cloud, some little way off the ground, approaching him. From this cloud there came a commanding voice. It asked him what he would rather die of – fever, dropsy or consumption? This strange and unpleasant question, asked in such a strange and unpleasant way, didn't seem to faze Mr Jones, however. He gave it some thought and then replied 'consumption' (ie tuberculosis). Apparently satisfied, the cloud went away and Mr Jones came over all sleepy. When he awoke he was ill – with consumption. A year and a day later he died, but not before he had had plenty of time to get all his affairs in order.

St. David's Cathedral in Pembrokeshire. According to legend St. David's prayers are responsible for the ghostly omens of death experienced by the Welsh